Creative Crafts for Creative Hands

FRESH FLOWER
ARRANGING

CHARTWELL BOOKS
a division of Book Sales, Inc.
POST OFFICE BOX 7100
114 Northfield Avenue
Edison, NJ 08818-7100

CLB 4126
© 1995 CLB Publishing, Godalming, Surrey
Printed and bound in Proost N.V., Belgium
All rights reserved
ISBN 0-7858-0124-3

CLB 4126
This edition published in 1995 by Tiger Books International PLC, London
© 1995 CLB Publishing, Godalming, Surrey
Printed and bound in Proost, N.V. Belgium
All rights reserved
ISBN 1-85501-593-5

Managing Editor: Jo Finnis
Editors: Sue Wilkinson; Geraldine Christy
Jacket and prelim design: Art of Design
Typesetting: Litho Link Ltd, Welshpool, Powys
Production: Ruth Arthur; Sally Connolly; Neil Randles; Karen Staff; Jonathan Tickner; Matthew Dale
Director of Production: Gerald Hughes

Photographers
Jacket Steve Tanner/Eaglemoss; Jacket flap; Simon Page-Ritchie/Eaglemoss; Title Page; Simon Page Ritchie/Eaglemoss; 9 100 Idees; 10 John Suett/Eaglemoss; 11 Steve Tanner/Eaglemoss; 12 100 idees; 13 Zefa; 15 Garden Picture Library; 16 Elizabeth Whiting Associates; 17-18 Modes et Travaux; 19 Araidne Holland; 20 Steve Tanner/Eaglemoss; 22 Elizabeth Whiting Associates; 23-26 Elizabeth Whiting Associates; 27-30 Simon Page-Ritchie/Eaglemoss; 31 Elizabeth Whiting Associates; 32 Boys Syndication; 34(t) Elizabeth Whiting Associates; 34(b) Insight Picture Library; 35 Simon Page-Ritchie/Eaglemoss; 37-38 Simon Page-Ritchie/Eaglemoss; 39 Elizabeth Whiting Associates; 40 Lamontagne; 41 Robert Harding Syndication/IPC Magazines; 42 Elizabeth Whiting Associates; 44 Elizabeth Whiting Associates; 45-46 Robert Harding Syndication/IPC Magazines; 47 Houses and Interiors; 48 Robert Harding Syndication/IPC Magazines; 49 100 Idees; 50 (t) Insight Picture Library; 50 (c) Insight Picture Library; 50 (b) Lamontagne; 51 Garden Picture Library; 53-55 Steve Tanner/Eaglemoss; 56 Elizabeth Whiting Associates; 57 Elizabeth Whiting Associates; 58-60 Steve Tanner/Eaglemoss

Illustrators
10-11 Elisabeth Dowle; 14 Elisabeth Dowle; 16 Elisabeth Dowle; 18 Elisabeth Dowle; 21-22 Michael Shoebridge; 24-26 Elisabeth Dowle; 28-30 Elisabeth Dowle; 33 Michael Shoebridge; 36 Elisabeth Dowle; 38 Elisabeth Dowle; 40 Elisabeth Dowle; 42-44 Michael Shoebridge; 47 Michael Shoebridge; 49 Jenny Abbott/Garden Studio; 52 Elisabeth Dowle; 54-55 Michael Shoebridge; 58-60 Michael Shoebridge

Creative Crafts for Creative Hands

FRESH FLOWER
ARRANGING

*How to make beautiful gifts and objects for the home,
from basic techniques to finishing touches.*

CHARTWELL
BOOKS, INC.

Contents

Preparing cut flowers

▲ Market fresh
Fresh flowers can add a breath of fresh air and a welcome splash of colour to your home. A few minutes spent preparing cut flowers guarantees that you enjoy their beauty for as long as possible. Adding a fresh look to your home for many days.

Whether you buy cut flowers, harvest them from your garden, or receive them as a gift, you'll want them to remain fresh and attractive for as long as possible. The length of time cut flowers will stay fresh varies from type to type: fresias, for example, will last about a week, while flowers such as carnations will last for up to three weeks, if cared for properly.

When buying or picking, it's important to know the difference between a young flower and an over-mature one. But how you prepare or condition it for display, and the care you give it once arranged, will determine whether it stays attractive for its full natural life-span or dies prematurely.

The techniques are quick and easy and no special tools are needed. Methods vary slightly from one type of flower to another, but they're based on common sense. for the best results, condition as soon as possible after cutting or buying keep the stem taking up water and food, and keep the vase water clean.

The method you choose to prepare the cut flower will be determined by the type of stem it has. For instance the hard woody stem of a rose needs different handling to the milky soft stem of a poppy. It is easy to identify the type of stem by just looking at it – it will be woody, hollow or milky, or have nodes, like the stems of carnations. The most important thing to remember is that each type of stem has slightly different preparation techniques

If you are harvesting flowers from your garden for indoor display rather than purchasing cut flowers, be sure to carry out your picking either early in the morning or at the end of the day. Immediately after harvesting, set about the preparatory treatment appropriate to the plant type (see pages 10–11).

Re-cutting stems

Woody stems

Tough stems

Stems with nodes

Carnations and pinks have enlarged joints (nodes) growing at intervals along the stems, which cannot take up water. Re-cut the stems between the two lowest nodes.

Bulb stems

The white lower end of the stems of plants such as tulips, lilies and daffodils, are unable to take up water. Therefore, cut the stem off where it begins to turn green.

After the initial cutting of the plants, re-cut the bottom of the stems at an angle. This will create the largest possible surface area for the uptake of water.

Ideally, the re-cutting of the stems should take place under water. But if there are any difficulties in doing this, quickly plunge the stem in water immediately after cutting. This will stop any air locks forming, which would otherwise prevent water reaching the flower.

Vertically split the bottom 1in (2.5cm) of woody stemmed plants, such as roses or forsythia. This helps in the uptake of water, so the plant will last longer.

Tough stemmed plants, like chrysanthemums, should be treated in the same way as those with woody stems. Another way to promote the uptake of water is to scrape the stem ends.

tip

Rose thorns
Thorny rose stems are difficult to work with and awkward to insert in displays. Florists use special thorn removers, but sharp scissors will also work well; draw the sharp edge along the stem or snip off thorns individually.

Woody/tough stems
Examples: roses; forsythia; chrysanthemums

Stems with nodes
Examples: carnations; pinks

Bulb stems
Examples: irises; tulips; hyacinths lilies; daffodils

Hollow stems

Milky stems

Boiling stems

Stripping leaves

Delphiniums, lupins and large dahlias have hollow stems. Turn the flower upside down, fill the stem to the top with water, then place in water. Water will continue to be drawn up the stem, to replace that lost by transpiration (the process of losing water vapour as the plant 'breathes').

Some plants, such as poppies, euphorbias and poinsettias, ooze a milky fluid (known as latex) when they are cut. To prevent this happening, hold the cut end of the stem near to a lit match or gas flame for just a few seconds. Then plunge the singed end of the stem in cold water.

This can be done instead of singeing. It also helps to soften woody stems, in plants such as roses, lilacs and hollyhocks, therefore improving water uptake. Carefully place a towel over the top to protect the flowers from the steam; or cover with a paper bag. Place the cut ends of the stems in 1in (2.5cm) of boiling water for one minute; then fill the container with cold water and leave for several hours.

Any lower leaves, which would be submerged in vase water, must be removed, or they will soon rot – not only making the water stale but also spoiling the effect of the display.

The leaves of dahlias and lilacs look dull and deprive the flowers of water. Chrysanthemum, lily and alstroemaria leaves die before the flowers and can spoil a display. Remove these, along with any leaves that hide the flowers.

Hollow stems
Examples: delphiniums; large dahlias; tulips

Milky stems
Examples: euphorbias; poppies; poinsettias

Pricking stems

Air bubbles can become trapped in the stems of some flowers, including tulips and polyanthus, preventing the uptake of water. To remove the air bubbles, use a needle or pin to prick the stem just beneath the flower heads. The plant can then take a long drink.

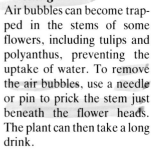

The long drink

Once you have finished the initial preparation, relevant to the type of flowers you are working with, you need to make sure that the plant takes a long drink.

Place the stem in a deep container of water for several hours – or, better still, overnight. This completes the conditioning process and makes the material turgid and ready for arranging.

Straightening stems

The stems of several flowers, such as tulips and anemones, elongate after being cut and curve towards the light. This can be used as a feature: otherwise, to straighten the stems, roll them in newspaper and place in deep water for several hours or overnight.

11

Removing stamens

The bright orange pollen on the stamens of the lily family can stain the petals, your hands, clothes and tablecloths. As this natural dye is very difficult to remove, it is, therefore, a good idea to remove the stamens immediately.

Some florists snip off the stamens during conditioning; but if not, use a pair of manicure scissors to trim them off this does the job just as well.

Reviving wilted flowers

Certain flowers, such as roses, wilt prematurely. If this occurs, re-cut the stem ends and place them in a deep vase of hand-hot water; or place in 1in (2.5cm) of boiling water for a minute, protecting the bloom, and follow with a long drink. Alternatively, cut the stems and submerge the entire flower in luke-warm water for a few hours, the bath-tub is the best place for this. Hydrangeas, violets and most foliage can be sub-merged for several hours to revive them.

Caring for displays

There are many ingenious tips which you can use to help prolong the life of fresh flower arrangements.

For a start, you should check water levels daily and top up as needed – especially 'heavy drinkers', such as tulips, arum lilies and anemones. If the flowers have been arranged in a florist's foam block, water until the excess overflows into the base.

Change the water in the container every 3–4 days, or once a week for water containing cut flower food. Thoroughly scrub the container between water changes, to prevent bacteria growing and dislodge any bacteria, which has already grown.

Use sachets of cut flower food in vase water. The sachets also contain an anti-bacterial agent, which helps to keep the water fresh. Or use carbonated lemo-nade instead of water; the citric acid in the lemonade kills bacteria and the sugar feeds the flowers; alternatively, put a few drops of bleach and a pinch of sugar in the vase water.

Keep displays away from direct heat, such as radiators; draughts, such as windows and air conditioners; and direct sunlight – all of which dehydrate flowers and cause them to wilt quite quickly.

In hot weather, or in centrally heated rooms, mist spray hydrangeas, violets, rhododendrons, and thin-leaved foliage, such as ferns. Do not spray near valuable furniture, as water can stain!

Every few days, re-cut the stems of long-lived flowers, such as chrysanthe-mums and roses. Remove any dead or discoloured flowers and foliage.

Spring flower arrangements

After the dark days of winter, with flowers scarce in the garden and costly in the shops, the arrival of spring is like a breath of fresh air. Local shops and stalls are full of cheap and cheerful daffodils and tulips, and the more expensive but longer lasting and fragrant hyacinths. Why not treat yourself to a couple of spring bunches? They look lovely displayed on their own, or for a personal touch, combined with forget-me-nots, garden foliage such as ivy, or branches of pussy willow or forsythia.

Tulips and freesias

Yellow and purple can look strident together, but here, pale yellow freesias and milky purple tulips, with darker purple inside, create a pleasant contrast,

▲ *Scented arrangement* The freesias add a sweet smell to a spring posy of tulips.

with green tulip leaves adding a cool, transitional tone. Freesias are sold all year round, but their pale colours fit easily into spring displays and they provide spring-like fragrance as well. Instead of yellow, you could use white freesias or, for a more subtle display, pale lavender ones, with purple tulips.

For a festive look, combine mixed-colour freesias and bright red or yellow tulips, or mixed tulips from the garden. Double tulips and fringed, multi-colour Fantasy and Parrot tulips are more expensive, and may have to be ordered from the florist in advance, but would

make a memorable dinner-party centrepiece. A simple china container is shown, but you could put these flowers in a white fluted soufflé dish or a plain round bowl. Turn the container continually as you insert the flowers to make sure it is arranged in a balanced way when viewed from all sides.

Freesia know-how
Buy freesias with the lowest flower open, and the buds above it just showing colour. This means they last longer.

A formal spring arrangement

This front-facing, triangle-shaped display features mixed daffodils and narcissi, peach and yellow double tulips, white freesias and hyacinths, forsythia, variegated euonymus, alder branches, laurustinus and red-foliaged berberis. All but the alder, berberis and euonymus are available from florists, and if these are not available you can substitute florist's curly willow branches and eucalyptus. Few florists sell mixed bunches of daffodils and narcissi so, if you don't grow them, you can use two or even one variety, such as the delicate, multi-headed Tazetta narcissus shown. On a budget, buy single yellow tulips.

Garden options include berberis, plain or variegated ivy or elaeagnus. For an oriental effect, substitute branches of angular, flowering quince or japonica with white or peach-coloured blossom for the forsythia.

A plain circular bowl has been used for this front-facing display and the florist's foam has been weighted to prevent the arrangement from overbalancing.

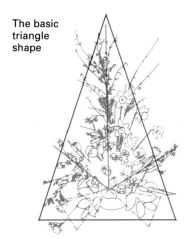

The basic triangle shape

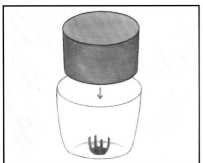

1 Start the display Use the container base as a template, pressing it into a block of florist's foam and then cut the block to fit. Saturate it in water. Place a wad of florist's mastic in the base of the container, press a florist's plastic prong or 'frog' on the mastic, then firmly impale the soaked block.

2 Setting the framework Insert two tall, multi-branched forsythia stems in the centre, angled slightly outwards to set the height. Cut an alder and two berberis slightly shorter than the forsythia and insert in front. Insert two shorter forsythia branches, angled, on either side, and one branch each of alder and berberis, slightly angled downwards each side.

3 Adding the foliage Create a foliage framework next. Insert two sprigs of laurustinus, angled down and out from the centre to cover the rim, and three branches of euonymus following the triangular shape, to reach half the height of the forsythia.

4 Daffodils and tulips Cut six daffodil and narcissus stems and two yellow tulips to graduated lengths, and insert the tallest two in the centre, fanning the shorter ones outwards, to fill out the triangle. Create a diagonal line of six peach tulips parallel to the left forsythia branch, and ending in the centre. Cluster six yellow tulips to the right of centre, again echoing the angle of the forsythia, and meeting the peach tulips in the centre.

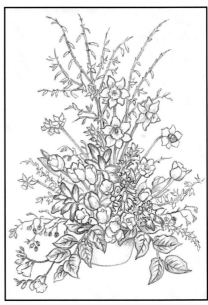

5 To form a focal point Tuck two hyacinth stems just to the right of centre. Cut four freesia stems to graduated lengths, and insert the two longest, angled down so the lowest one touches the table and the second just hovers above it. Insert the third freesia so the flowers just rest on the rim, and the fourth to touch the hyacinths. Check that none of the foam is showing, and adjust as necessary.

▲ **Formal yet fresh**
This arrangement is based on a triangle which means that most of the flowers and foliage are inserted in threes.

15

Garden ring

This winter-into-spring display combines the last snowdrops and Christmas roses with the first hyacinths and grape hyacinths. You could interpret it in all white, using white hyacinths and grape hyacinths, or substitute pink hyacinths, for a softly multi-coloured, pastel display. The Christmas roses will have to come from the garden, or use white or blue florist's anemones instead. Cut the ivy and polyanthus leaves shown from your garden or window box; buy pot plants and cut off a few sprigs and leaves; or use florist's leatherleaf fern, divided into sprigs.

In the 1940s and 1950s pottery ring vases were popular as a table centrepiece, and now they're making a comeback. You can also use a small china ring mould from the kitchen or a pre-formed, plastic-based florist's foam ring, which are cheap and come in several sizes.

▶ **Purple and white**
Hyacinths and snowdrops decorate this fragrant table centrepiece.

Looking after cut flowers
Re-cut the stems of florist-bought flowers when you get home, and place them in a tall container of water for several hours. Cut any white ends off bulb flowers, such as tulips and daffodils, otherwise they can't take up water. To keep the water clean and extend the life of the flowers, add a few drops of bleach.

1 To hold the display
Saturate the foam ring or fill a ring vase almost to the top with water. Insert sprigs of ivy and scented pelargonium or polyanthus leaves, arranging the ivy stems horizontally, so they cover the inner and outer rims.

2 Add the hyacinths
Cut the stems to the depth of the vase and insert four, evenly-spaced hyacinths.

3 Filling in the spaces
Divide the grape hyacinths and snowdrops into small clusters and insert at random in each section.

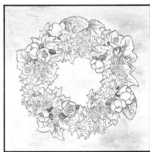

4 Finishing touch
Finally, insert the Christmas roses, two or three in a cluster and using the rest singly, to fill any gaps.

A fruit and flower display

An informal display of seasonal fruit, flowers and garden foliage is as much fun to create as it is enchanting to look at. It is also economical because you need few flowers, the leaves can be had for free and the fruit can be eaten later or, if artificial, put away for use again. The possible combinations are endless, so take your time and try out several 'raw ingredients' before finalizing your display; you're sure to get delectable results.

The fruit

Use fresh or artificial fruit, or a mixture of both. Artificial fruit, such as grapes, is probably more practical if you want the display to last as the fresh version is naturally short-lived. Choose good-quality fake fruit, since the display is seen at close range. With fresh fruit, such as apples, buy perfect specimens, under-ripe rather than at the peak of perfection.

You can even splash out and buy one

▲ Tasty centrepiece
Fruit, flowers and foliage, with their contrasting organic forms and strong natural colours, are ideal 'raw ingredients' for an impressive table display.

or two of the more exotic fruits that are now available in large supermarkets and fruiterers such as pomegranates, grenadines and tamarillos – try to include a range of shapes, colours and sizes.

17

The flowers

A delightful mixture of florist's and garden flowers is used in our display: hydrangea, tansy, a couple of huge florist's chrysanthemums and small spray chrysanthemums. Dahlias or gerberas could replace the large chrysanthemums; use spray carnations instead of the smaller chrysanthemums, and yarrow instead of the tansy.

For contrasting outline, dried spiraea flower spikes are used, but dried or fresh buddleia or hebe would be fine. The flowers are mostly yellow, in contrast with the fruit, but you could repeat the fruit colours or add sparkle with all-white blooms.

The foliage

The exact plant species are less important than a good range of colour, scale and shape. Oak leaves provide sculptural form and brown hues, but autumnal beech, hornbeam or bracken foliage are also attractive.

For our display, shiny laurel and cotoneaster leaves provide greenery, but mahonia, holly or elaeagnus are equally good. Try brilliant crimson fishbone cotoneaster, or larch, with its decorative cones. Although you could use florist's eucalyptus or fern, it's best to include a few 'natural' leaves, if only wild ivy or knotweed, or privet snipped from a hedge. Wash and dry all the foliage before using it.

The base

This display is in a plastic bowl within a stemmed, shallow, cut-glass compote dish, but a stemmed, flat cake stand would give the same effect. Avoid stemless bases, since the elegant effect of material trailing over the rim is lost; and deep-rimmed containers, which call for a different technique. Use plain glass, china, pottery or wood but avoid heavily decorated bases, which vie with their contents for attention.

Other equipment

A few other items are necessary for making a centrepiece such as this. A block of **florist's foam**, which should be soaked in cold water before use, is essential. You will also need **florist's mastic** – a sticky, clay-like substance that comes in a roll – and a plastic **florist's prong**, on which the block of foam is impaled.

These items are available from flower shops. Special-purpose plastic bowls and wires can also be purchased, but for this display any shallow, lightweight bowl would suffice, while toothpicks will do the job of florist's wire.

MAKING THE DISPLAY

▲ **Starting the arrangement**
The shallow bowl containing the foam will be completely concealed by the final arrangement.

1 Starting the display With a little florist's mastic attach the bowl to the centre of the base. With more mastic, fix a florist's prong to the bottom of the bowl. Cut florist's foam block to fit, saturate with water, and impale on the prong.

2 The foliage framework Using various leaves and spiraea spikes, build a collar round the bowl rim. Angle the stems down towards the front, up towards the back, radiating from a central point and overhanging the rim here and there. Rest some leaves directly on the base, fixed with a dab of mastic.

3 Positioning the fruit Fix a bunch of grapes to the foam block, using toothpicks or florist's wire bent into a U-shape. Trail another bunch of grapes over the rim, off-centre, resting the bulk on the base. Rest three fresh apples on the base, one between the bunches of grapes. Fix with mastic, if wished.

4 Positioning the flowers Cut the stems of two large chrysanthemums to 5cm (2in) and insert diagonally on either side of the central grapes. Fix a hydrangea between the two bunches of grapes, the flower heads almost touching the foam. Insert small flowers randomly, tucked into the centre, and filling gaps.

Easter flowers

Easter is a wonderful time for fresh flowers. Daffodils and tulips are readily available in most florists and these can be added to buds and greenery from the garden to make stunning displays, which don't cost the earth.

It is also a good time to try decorating your home with alternative flower arrangements such as the two overleaf. For example you can bring a refreshing softness to dried flower displays by supplementing them with parchment flowers. They come in very realistic colours, shapes and sizes so that at a glance they look like real blooms. The step by step arrangement overleaf would make a stunning centre-piece for an entrance hall and would be seen and admired by everyone who calls.

Poppy seed heads, dried flowers and grasses form the basis of this display but for a lasting effect the dried and parchment flowers used in the arrangement have been specially chosen so that they never look out of season and are a perfect match for the room decorations. Make sure your choice of vase also matches and is in overall proportion with the arrangement, as there is nothing worse than a top heavy display.

This type of flower arrangement can of course be altered as often as you want. If, for example, after Easter, you want a simpler effect you could place the parchment irises in a tall vase and store the rest of the arrangement in a box for use with fresh greenery another time.

The delightful dining table centre-

▲ Tulips and twigs
Pale pink tulips, white hyacinths, grape hyacinths and apple blossom make up this stunning arrangement for Easter, which has been set in vases hidden inside a twiggy basket. If you are lucky this choice of blooms can be hand picked from your garden or supplemented with florist flowers.

piece on page 22 has been given an Easter theme by the addition of eggs in the terracotta pots. Designed to last for just a few hours, the arrangement can't be moved and is built up over a base of plates or saucers filled with saturated oasis. Take care to protect a polished table from water spills by covering it with a sheet of plastic.

19

MAKING THE DISPLAY

This stunning centrepiece is made from long lasting parchment flowers, dried flowers and grasses. The parchment flowers are often bought in a flat pack so they may need to be moulded into a lifelike form before use. Choose your vase and plant material carefully for a colour co-ordinated arrangement that will match the room where it is to be displayed.

▲ Paper perfection
This wonderful display of parchment and dried flowers will still look fresh months later when real flowers would have faded. No watering is necessary although you may need to reposition any knocked flowers.

Materials

6 paper irises 1 yellow, 1 white and 4 blue
1 paper wild rose white
1 paper poppy yellow
1 paper tea rose white
2 paper sprays of snapdragons, blue
6 dried poppy seed heads
10 dried achillea heads
bunch of dried barley grasses
bunch of foxtail millet
florists wire cutters
Vase and **dried florists foam**

20

1 Starting the arrangement Fill your vase to the rim with a single block of dry florist's foam. Then make an outline with the grasses and foxtail millet ensuring that the overall height of your arrangement is no more than twice the height of your vase.

2 Adding the irises Position and add the irises. Cut the stems with pliers or florists' wire cutters, to the required length. Bend and move stems and leaves gently to give a softer more natural look to the arrangement. Tweak the petals to achieve the effect you desire.

3 Adding other parchment flowers Position the white roses, the yellow poppy and blue snapdragon sprays as shown cutting and bending the stems as before, again tweak the petals if necessary, and ensure the flowers are secure in the dry florist's foam.

4 Finishing off the display When you have arranged all the parchment flowers fill in the areas between the blooms with the poppy seed heads and achillea being careful to keep the original balanced shape. You can also add more grasses if needed at this stage.

21

AN EASTER DELIGHT

Materials
Sprigs of cherry and apple blossom
Bunches of grape hyacinths, primroses and anemones
Bun and sphagnum moss
Sprigs of ivy
Quails eggs
Three saucers and blocks of florist's foam to fit saucers
Florist's wire and two terracotta pots

On Easter Day a special table decoration can add to the enjoyment of the family celebration. This lovely spring garden arrangement, with its half concealed treasures of eggs, would be fun to make with the children. Instead of quails eggs in the little terracotta pots, you could dye ordinary eggs with food colouring or if you prefer substitute sugar or chocolate ones. The arrangement is made on the table so you may wish to protect it with a sheet of polythene before starting work.

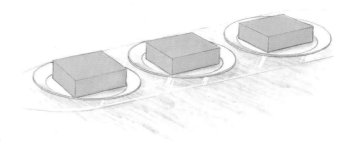

1 Making the base Space three saucers about 20cm (10in) apart along the centre of the table in a fairly straight line. Place a saturated block of florist's foam in each saucer and top up with water.

2 Building up foliage Cover florist's foam with flowers, clustering them rather like in a garden. To create an asymmetric effect start at the far end saucer and work towards the centre. Pile bun moss and sphagnum moss between saucers to create height and the effect of a landscape adding more sprigs of foliage between the mosses.

tip

Looking good
The flowers should be secured in the moist foam to keep them fresh.

3 Adding pots Rest the small terracotta pots on their sides, towards one end banking them with moss to keep them stable. Insert flowers and eggs into the pots.

4 Finishing off Break up any harsh lines in the display with ivy tendrils. Tuck in any edges of the plastic sheet and hide as necessary with ivy.

▼ *Eggstra special* The eggs add a superb finishing touch to this splendid Easter arrangement, which is unbelievably quick and easy to make.

Spring and summer colour

The most wonderful aspect of arranging cut flowers in the home in late spring and early summer is the sheer abundance of choice and material. Flowers and foliage in the garden are there for the picking, and cutting them for the house will benefit the garden as well. Picking flowers such as roses and sweet peas regularly encourages them to bloom even more, in the same way that deadheading does. Trimming sprigs or branches of foliage or flowering shrubs can keep them looking compact and improve the look of the garden, at the same time as providing background material or bulk for your indoor flower arrangements.

In florist's shops, prices tend to come down in spring and summer, as the variety of form and colour increases. The wide range of inexpensive, informal flowers and foliage available means that you can create generous, dramatic displays wherever you live without any hint of pretension or extravagance. The only problem, it it is a problem, is being spoiled for choice!

In the pink

One colour schemes, based on shades of a single hue, are easy to create and restful to the eye. They also emphasize the variation of flower forms that are all too easily 'lost' in flamboyant multi-coloured arrangements. In this pretty all-pink display, a potted azalea adds fullness and contrasting texture.

Incorporating flowers or foliage from houseplants is an easy way to fill a large

▲Single colour
A potted azalea is the starting point for this all-pink display.

container, and a perfectly acceptable short-cut from taking all the plants for the arrangements from the garden.

Flowers and foliage
You will need a potted azalea in flower, three or four hyacinths, amaryllis, parrot tulips and several single tulips. For greenery add a bunch of tulip leaves, laurustinus leaves and dill.

Materials
The arrangement is set in a bowl which is large enough to hide the azalea pot. You will also need small-mesh wire netting and a plastic bag.

1 Wrap the azalea pot in a plastic bag to prevent waterlogging. Place in the bowl, slightly to one side; if it sits too low, raise it on a piece of wire netting. Firmly pack the rest of the bowl with crumpled wire mesh netting. Fill the bowl with water, being careful not to overfill.

2 Cut the tulip flower stems low down to separate the foliage. Cut off the white lower stem. Use the tulip and laurustinus leaves and dill to hide the mesh. Build a low framework, starting at the outer edge and working in. It should only protrude about 5cm (2in) above the bowl, but should extend out to about twice the bowl's width.

3 Cut the white ends off the hyacinth stems and insert in a group, next to the azalea. Insert the parrot tulips, cut to various lengths, in a loose group, opposite the azalea, putting shorter stems towards the centre. Insert a loose group of single tulips between the two. It is easier to place a single flower each time. Finally, insert the amaryllis low down and off centre.

Rich and cool

Regal purple and cool, pristine white are combined in this informal all-round, low display, ideal for a coffee table or as the centre-piece for a dining table. This arrangement is easier to compile in springtime.

Flowers and foliage

A bunch of amaryllis, small bunch of bluebells, three or four anemones, jasmine, trachelium, deutzia and viburnum foliage and flowers and ivy are the main elements of this arrangement but only tiny sprigs of jasmine, deutzia, and viburnum are used. Similar material could easily be substituted, or you could omit some of them altogether and use more of others. Even sprigs of ordinary hedging, such as privet, berberis or yew, would do nicely.

Materials

A blue and white or plain white shallow bowl filled with small-mesh wire netting is used to hold the arrangement.

1 Crumple the wire mesh netting loosely into a ball. Place the netting in the bowl, then fill the bowl three quarters full with water. Carefully cut the trachelium stems short and insert them into the bowl, level with the rim. You'll find that their flat heads will help to hold the other flowers in place.

2 Cut the remaining flower stems slightly longer, so the flower heads will rest on the trachelium. Then fill approximately half of the bowl with tightly bunched white anemones, ending at the centre line and building up a gentle dome shape by adding more anemones at the centre and less at the outside.

3 Fill one quarter with tightly bunched purple anemones and bluebells, and the remaining quarter with white amaryllis. Tuck in sprigs of viburnum, jasmine, ivy and deutzia or similar material, to fill any gaps, add contrast and break up the outline. Again, try to build up the display towards the centre by packing the flowers more tightly in the middle.

tip

Picking bluebells
When picking bluebells, always cut the flower off above the white, lower portion of the stem. Leaving this part attached to the bulb helps it build up reserves for next year's flowering.

▲ *A hint of purple*
A couple of glorious white amaryllis blooms are the focal point of this arrangement. Areas of deep purple and white anemones are used to balance the display with trails of ivy. They also help break up the solid outline. Other coloured flowers could also be used if you prefer.

Freshen up
To keep the cut azalea fresh looking, lightly mist spray it daily, and try to keep it in a room where the temperature is cool.

Summer symmetry

This informal display, based on a symmetrical triangle, captures all the generosity and abundance of summer, while mirroring the symmetry of the décor. The predominant pink theme is enlivened by crimson antirrhinums and cerise and orange celosia, or cockscomb, a Victorian favourite. These intense col-

ours also create a sense of depth in the shallow, front-facing arrangement. Foliage and flowers on and overhanging the chest are a lovely touch.

Flowers and foliage

This pink arrangement includes stargazer lilies, azalea branches, rowan branches, phlox, antirrhinums, celosia, a few spray

carnations, a bunch of large-flowered roses, and multiflora roses.

Materials

The arrangement fills a plastic-lined, woven twig basket into which is placed a saturated florist's foam block, held in place with florist's mastic and a florist's prong.

1 Place a blob of mastic in the base of the basket. Press the prong into it, then impale the foam block on the prong. Use 3 equal-length rowan branches to set the height and width of the display. Insert phlox and antirrhinums of a similar length to reinforce the height and width, and build up mass.

2 Insert large-flowered roses vertically in the middle, at two-thirds the rowan's height, then add a column of azalea branches below. Cut the celosia stems short and use them to make a tightly packed, diagonal band. Again, it is easier to make the arrangement if you place each flower in position singly.

3 Use the lilies, shorter stemmed rowan, phlox and antirrhinums, spray carnations and arching branches of multiflora roses to fill the space inside the imaginary triangle, building up density towards the centre. Keep the outline loose, and face some flowers sideways, for variety.

Table swags

This delightful floral swag will make an impressive table decoration for any special occasion. Based on a chicken wire tube, filled with moss, it is surprisingly easy to make. Use any flowers in season, either limiting your colour scheme to two or three shades – cream and yellow are used here – or create a glorious swag full of the colours of a summer garden.

Materials

A length of **chicken wire** at least 1.75m x 30cm (6 x 1ft).
A long piece of **string**.
Wire cutters.
Enough **sphagnum moss** to make a roll 1.75m long and about 10cm (4in) wide.

75cm (2½ft) **gardening wire**.
18m (20ft) of white **florist's ribbon** 5cm (2in) wide.
Water sprayer.
Large feature flowers such as a head of **amaryllis lilies**.
3 stems of medium-sized flowers such as **yellow lilies** – *Lilium hollandicum* 'Destiny'.
Smaller flowers such as 2 stems of **white chrysanthemums** and 2 stems of pale yellow spiky **spider flowered chrysanthemums**.
Medium-sized foliage such as **variegated euonymus** and **eucalyptus hedging** or **tree pieces** such as apple and cherry.
Small scale foliage such as **ivy** and *Cotoneaster horizontalis*.

▲ A flower-filled swag
Restricting the colours of the flowers can be most effective, and the colours can be chosen to match the decor of the room, the colours of the table linen or, if used for a wedding, the bride's bouquet.

27

MAKING THE SWAG

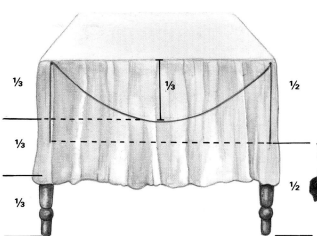

1 Measuring the table With the cloth you are planning to use laid on the table, measure from the table top to the floor. Divide this measurement into half and thirds. Use a piece of string to calculate the length of the swag. Pin it to the corners of the table so that the ends of the string hang halfway and the centre of the dip is a third of the way down. Mark the fixing positions on the string.

4 Shaping the swag Leave the wire tube in water to soak through completely; then leave to drain until the water stops dripping.

Using the string as a guide, measure from each end to the fixing positions and twist a 30cm (12in) length of garden wire round the tube at each of these points and form into hanging loops. The wire loops are used to hang the swag on the table so they must be securely fixed. Bend the ends of the tube down and shape the centre portion into a gentle curve.

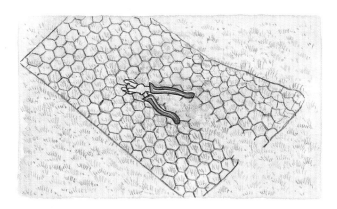

2 Cutting the chicken wire Use the string to determine the length of the wire and cut a strip to this measurement and 30cm (12in) wide.

5 Working on the swag It is easiest to work on the swag if it is hanging up. Knock two nails, the required distance apart, into a stout piece of wood. Place the piece of wood across the backs of two chairs and hang the swag from them. You may need to weight the chair seats with books. Otherwise, lay the swag on the floor making sure it is in the correct shape for the table.

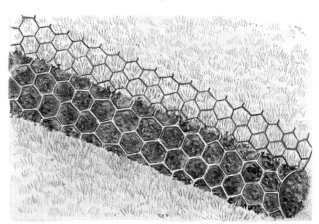

3 Making the roll Place the moss along the centre of the wire and, beginning at one end, fold the wire over the moss to create a roll. Fix the cut edges together as you go, completely enclosing the moss. Bend over the ends of the tube to prevent the moss falling out. Squeeze the wire tube together so that the moss is really secure inside.

6 Inserting the foliage Cut the euonymus and eucalyptus or cherry and apple twigs into 15-20cm (6-8in) lengths. Starting from the centre, insert them into the wire-covered moss so that the sprigs face away from the centre. As you move along the swag, place each piece behind the last so that the foliage already inserted overlaps the new piece.

7 **Balancing the leaf materials** Step back from the work from time to time to check that the different types of foliage are evenly distributed along the swag and the two sides are balanced. All the shaping is done with the foliage; as you work up to the bend of the swag, start using the smaller-leaved sprigs so that the outline narrows at this point. Then, working down the outer tails, start using the larger foliage at the top tapering off with the smaller leaves at the ends.

8 **Fixing the swag to the table** Before adding any of the flowers the swag should be fixed in position on the table. If you are using an old or a trestle table, the wire hangers can be fixed by stapling through the cloth into the wood. If, however, you do not want to mark the cloth or the table, pin the wire hangers to the cloth using several safety pins. The pins will be hidden by the ribbon rosette. The cloth will need to be weighted throughout the event but while you are working you can use several heavy books to prevent it slipping off.

11 **Wiring the amaryllis** The centrepiece of the arrangement is an amaryllis. The flower heads are removed from the stem and wired for support. Cut a piece of wire 20cm (8in) long and insert through the base of the flower. Bend both ends down like a hairpin.

Twist a second 20cm (8in) length of wire round the base of the flower and down the stem.

12 **Inserting the amaryllis** Use the wire stem to insert the heads into the centre of the swag, tilting one or two heads upwards.

13 **Hiding the wire hangers** Place a ribbon rosette over the fixings and let the tails curl and hang down each side attractively (see page 30). Give the final arrangement a spray with water to keep it fresh.

9 **Inserting the flowers** Start at the centre and insert a ring of chrysanthemums to cover the bare patch where the foliage divides. Continue inserting flowers along the swag and down the tails, checking from time to time that they are balanced on each side.

10 **Adding the lilies** Cut the stems of the yellow lilies to 15-20cm (6-8in) and insert them in the same way. This is an informal arrangement so do not place the individual flowers too regularly, one or two clumps as well as single flowers look attractive. The table swag will be viewed from above as well as from the front so make sure some of the flower heads are placed along the top of the central draped portion.

Guidelines for garlands
Storing the swag Once all the foliage has been inserted the swag can be stored for a couple of days without drooping. The flowers can be inserted on the day, ensuring they stay fresh for the special occasion.

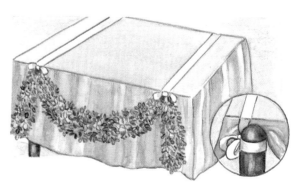

Fixing the swag with ribbon The swag can be hung on the front of the table using two lengths of florist's ribbon. Tie one end of the ribbon around the rear leg (anti-clockwise on the right leg, facing the table, and clockwise on the left leg). Take the ribbon over the table and tie to the wire hangers. This method works best on a table which is set against a wall as the cloth will have to pass round the ribbon at the back.
Remove the pollen The pollen of some lilies can stain if you brush against them so snip off any pollen-laden stamens inside each flower as you work.

▼ *An interesting outline*
To achieve a charmingly natural look do not strive to make each side exactly the same. Add the odd twig or flower to break up the outline if it looks too planned.

MAKING A RIBBON ROSETTE

1 Measuring the ribbon Cut a 3m (10ft) length of ribbon for each rosette. Cut off 90cm (36in) for the tail and set this aside. Thread a needle with cotton to match the colour of the ribbon.

2 Making the rosette Make a loop about 10cm (4in) long at one end of the ribbon. Holding the loop together with your thumb and forefinger, make a similar loop slightly to the right.
  Continue making loops, holding them at the centre and moving round in a circle. When the circle is complete, wind the end into a small loop at the centre.

3 Holding the layers Use a needle and cotton to stitch through all layers to hold, then fold the tail in half and stitch to the back of the rosette.
  Cut the ends of the tail into a V or an angle and pin or stitch the rosette in position on the swag.

Extra tails
For an extra special occasion you could split each ribbon tail into four separate ribbons. Divide the ribbon into four at the end, and then cut upwards. Each section can then be curled individually.

▼ *Hidden fixings* Apart from looking pretty, the ribbon rosette will hide the wire hanging hooks and fixings at each end of the table. Curl the tails by running the ribbon firmly between your thumb and the blade of a pair of scissors.

Mid-summer displays

The best time to create extravagant flower arrangements is summer. During this season the enormous range of flowers and foliage available from gardens and flower shops means you can mix and match blooms, to make generous displays which would be out of the question at any other time of the year.

Many favourite cottage garden flowers, such as sweet peas, are grown commercially so you can create a fresh-from-the-garden display even if you don't have a garden. Other good sources of flowers are fêtes and country shows which provides a great excuse for a weekend outing as well as offering you the chance to pick up more unusual and inexpensive foliage.

You can base the colour scheme of your display on mixed pastels or if you prefer use a bolder mix of flowers. Alternatively, use a single colour theme

▲ Summer medley
Philadelphus, larkspur, lady's mantle and old-fashioned and species roses are all combined with variegated dogwood in this side-table display.

such as white or even tints of pink and red. A more sophisticated option is an all-green display with green flowers, seed heads and foliage all in subtly different hues.

Inspirational material

Flowers Certain blooms such as old-fashioned roses, peonies, delphiniums and campanulas have an inherent quality of summer, which helps to set the tone for a display, especially if some of the other flowers included, such as chrysanthemums, are not seasonal. Later summer flowers include hydrangeas, red-hot poker and dahlias as well as the perpetual blooms of hybrid tea and floribunda roses. As a rule, any combination of flowers that work well growing in close proximity will look good in a cut flower display.

A huge bowl of one type of flower or very similar blooms such as mixed cultivars of old-fashioned roses, can be effective, or a mix that draws visual strength from deliberately contrasting shapes, sizes and textures.

Foliage Garden foliage is a great summer bonus. Even plants as modest as privet or periwinkle can provide the bulk and green backdrop that transform a few flowers into a lush display. Coloured foliage such as variegated dogwood or purple sage can add depth to an arrangement and act as a visual bridge between flowers and greenery. Less exciting foliage such as eucalyptus, smilax and leather-leaf fern also look good, if used informally and generously. Pruning from hedges can also prove useful, but if you need to buy foliage from florists, avoid dark, mournful evergreens, such as box and cypress.

MAKING THE ARRANGEMENT

This front-facing display is loosely based on a low triangle. It features a mixture of summer flowers and foliage building up to a dense centre. If you use florists' roses, try to choose forms with flatter blooms that will open reliably and are long-lasting; ask your florist if you are unsure. Traditional long-stemmed rose buds often

wilt before they open. At a pinch, you can gently force long-stemmed rose buds open by placing the stems in warm water in a steamy room.

Silver foliage adds a special lightness, but is rarely available commercially. As an alternative, you could ask your florist to order white-variegated ivy, narrow-leaved eucalyptus and bear grass.

The slightly raised bowl used in this display creates enough height for the material to arch gracefully. To get a similar effect, place a flat bowl on an upturned saucer or shallow dish, but make sure they are stable. If in doubt, secure them with florist's mastic before starting to arrange the flowers.

Materials

Bowl, florist's foam, prong and **mastic**
5-6 stems of *Artemisia ludoviciana*
1 bunch **pink sweet peas**
2-4 branches of **flowering honeysuckle**
9-12 veronica flowers
7-8 marjoram flowers
8 deep pink roses
6 pale pink roses
5 stems **alchemilla**
2 stems **silver-leaved cineraria**
3-4 stems **gypsophila**
2 stems **flowering jasmine**
1 bunch **lavender**

1 Start the display Place florist's mastic in a cross shape in the base of the bowl. Press a prong firmly in the middle of the mastic. Then impale foam, cut to fit the bowl snugly, on to the prong. The foam should project 2.5-5cm (1-2in) above the rim of the bowl.

2 Setting the framework Place a tall artemisia stem centrally and well back, to set the height. Use two sweet pea stems and one large honeysuckle branch on the right, and three veronica stems on the left, to set the width. Insert four artemisia, three marjoram and five veronica stems as intermediate markers. Bring some forward and angled down, to break the rim line.

3 Beginning infill Cut the eight deep pink roses to varying lengths and form them into a sinuous 'S' shape down the centre. Place two pale pink roses at a low angle to one side, and four pale pink roses to the other side to give the arrangement depth. Insert the remaining sweet peas angled outwards and downwards to form three prongs, with a tight central cluster.

4 Building up density Add the remaining marjoram, honeysuckle and veronica stems to increase density, especially towards the middle. Add five alchemilla stems, for colour and textural contrast. Place two sprigs of silver-leaved cineraria on either side of the centre, to informally frame the roses.

◄ *Scented splendour* Old-fashioned roses and sweet peas form the central theme of this wonderful summer arrangement. The sprigs of lavender, jasmine and honeysuckle all add extra fragrance to the display. If you want the floral arrangement to fit in with your interior you could change the colour of the roses.

5 Finishing off Use sprigs of gypsophila to create a lacy contrast and fill any gaps. Insert sprigs of jasmine, some long, some short, to overhang the rim, and a bunch of lavender slightly off centre. As you proceed, check the display from the sides as well as the front, to ensure an even build-up.

If you choose your flowers carefully you can bring those wonderful summer scents indoors.

Stunning extras

You needn't confine yourself to the garden or florist for your raw material. The fresh vegetable department of your local supermarket can provide curled, crisped and oak-leaf lettuces, for use as cut foliage in flower arrangements.

In your own garden, dig up any lettuces that have gone to seed, roots and all, and wash the soil away. You'll be surprised how long-lasting they are when used in a floral display.

From the herb garden, pick large sprigs of parsley, dill or fennel for adding a delicate touch. Purple sage and yellow variegated sage are also attractive in floral displays.

Fresh nasturtium flowers can be used in salads, so you should be able to obtain them at the local delicatessen. You could also float them in a shallow bowl of water, for a special table centrepiece.

▶ Cool, calm and collected
Goldenrod, arum lilies, green flowers of Viburnum opulus and alstroemerias repeat the colour theme of the vase.

▼ Fun with foliage
A dish of blue rue and red lettuce accompanies a typical summery mixture of pale yellow roses, acid green euphorbia bracts, and rue, purple sage and periwinkle foliage.

Shaped arrangements

Florist's foam is an easy material to cut or build up into shapes. You can carve a small shape out of a single block or use two or three pieces, bound together, to make up a larger piece which is then trimmed to shape.

Some florists will supply pre-shaped foam blocks in a limited range of designs, but it is fun to make your own.

A floral heart

Three oblong blocks of florist's foam have been bound together and cut out in the shape of a heart. Make the finished shape to fit a large, flat dish or, if you

prefer, cut a heart-shaped piece of thick card and cover it with foil and place the drained arrangement on this to prevent it marking the table or cloth.

Using the basic technique given here you can create arrangements in almost any shape. Rings, triangles, letters or a number for a special birthday party – there are endless possibilities.

If the arrangement is to go on a table it will be seen close up so try to keep the scale of the flowers and foliage small and in proportion to each other – avoid using large bulky leaves or big bold blooms that will obscure the shape.

▲ Heart of roses
This lovely flower arrangement is the perfect centrepiece for a special occasion, like a wedding, or just to adorn your table on a summer day. Roses in shades of pink are featured in this heart, but you could opt for yellow or peach coloured roses.

Materials

A sheet of **graph** or **squared paper**, a piece of **card** and a sheet of **tin foil**.

A green **florist's foam block** measuring 23cm x 11.5cm x 8cm (9in x 4½in x 3in).

A reel of **florist's foam tape** in white or green and a green **florist's cane**.

A sharp **kitchen knife** and **florist's scissors**.

A selection of foliage, including **rosemary**, **lavender**, **ivy**, **senecio** and **euphorbia**. 12 pink **rosebuds**, 6 stems of pink **spray carnations**, a small bunch of **gypsophila**.

MAKING A HEART SHAPED ARRANGEMENT

1 Make a pattern Draw a heart shape on the graph paper. To ensure it is symmetrical, fold in half and cut along one line.

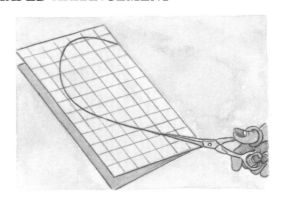

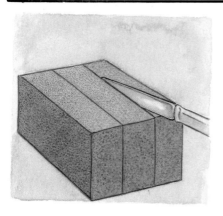

2 Prepare the block Cut the foam block lengthways into three even pieces using a sharp kitchen knife.

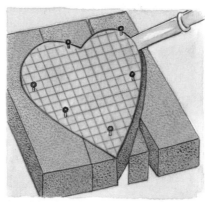

3 Cut out the shape Place the foam blocks side by side and pin the heart pattern to the block. Cut around the shape with the kitchen knife.

4 Bind it together Use florist's tape to hold the blocks together. A couple of florist's canes inserted widthways will also help keep the blocks still. Place the heart shape in water until it is soaked through.

5 Prepare the foliage Cut the ivy into 8cm (3in) pieces and the rest of the foliage into 5cm (2in) sprigs. Place the heart shape on a tray to work on and insert the pieces on the front and sides of the heart. The ivy works well following the shape of the sides if you insert both ends into the block. Alternate the types of foliage so that it is well mixed.

6 Insert the flowers The roses are the main flowers so place them first – one in the centre and the others spaced out over the heart. Fill the remaining spaces with carnations. Then, add sprigs of gypsophila to soften the outline.

Stand back from time to time to check the balance of the flowers and that the outline of the heart shape is still there.

7 Place the arrangement If the final arrangement is to stand on a plate there is no need to drain the oasis. If, however, you wish to use it as the centrepiece of a dining table, cut out a card heart, slightly larger than the paper pattern, cover it with foil and then place the well-drained arrangement on it for the meal. To freshen the arrangement, place the florist's foam on a tray and add water; leave for about half an hour.

A floral ball

Wrapping small blocks of florist's foam in chicken wire makes the base for a hanging ball arrangement which will keep fresh for a few days as long as you keep it well watered. Hang it from the centre of an archway, in an alcove, the centre of a bay window or, on special occasions to decorate a marquee!

Materials

A block of **florist's foam** measuring 23cm x 11.5cm x 8cm (9in x 4½in x 3in).
A flat piece of **chicken wire** about 60cm (24in) square

Several lengths of **stub wire** for the hanging hook and bow.
Florist's scissors.
Sharp **kitchen knife**.
Wire cutters.
A **flower pot** or similar container to hold the arrangement when working on it.
A 1.8m (2yd) length of 2cm (¾in) **florist's ribbon** to match the flowers.
A selection of foliage, including **rosemary, lavender, ivy, senecio, euphorbia**.
6 stems white **spray chrysanthemums**, 6 stems white **spray carnations**, 10 stems of white **freesias** and 4 stems of white **Singapore orchids**.

▲ **Summer arrangement**
Hung over an archway, or in a doorway, this lovely floral arrangement adds a fresh, bright look to your home. If you are feeling creative why not make different shapes such as a bell, or a ring. To freshen up the flowers simply spray with a plant mister.

MAKING A FLORAL BALL

1 Cut up the foam Using a sharp kitchen knife, slice the florist's foam block into eight pieces.

2 Wrap with wire Place the blocks in a mound in the middle of the chicken wire and gently wrap the wire round the blocks. Aim for a ball shape about 20cm (8in) in diameter, adjusting the blocks before you have completely enclosed them. Turn sharp ends inwards and use cut ends of the chicken wire to secure it firmly to itself.

3 Add a hanging hook With the folded edge of the chicken wire at the top attach a hanging hook to hold the ball when the florist's foam is filled with water. Use two stub wires, wound together and fix them to each edge of the wire.

4 Soak the ball Leave the ball in water for half an hour then let it drain thoroughly before starting to decorate.

5 Insert the foliage Place the ball, hook downwards, in a container such as a flower pot and create a foliage framework. Insert sprigs 8cm (3in) long, spacing them randomly over the ball and making sure you have a good mix of the different types. Stand back occasionally to check the ball shape is even. Reserve some sprigs for the top.

6 Add the flowers Cut the flower heads or sprigs to the same length as the foliage. Start with the chrysanthemums, placing them evenly over the ball, well spaced so that there is plenty of room for the rest of the flowers. Keep a couple of heads for the top of the ball.

7 Fill in the gaps The carnations are next, use both buds and flowers to give variety. Finally, insert the freesias and orchids. If the sprays are long, snip off the end buds and try and use the curve of the spray to follow the ball's shape.

8 Cover the top To finish off the ball you will need to hang it from the hook. A rod placed over the bath is a good place to hang it while you are working. Insert the greenery first and then the flowers. Give the final arrangement a spray of water.

9 Add a bow Take a 1.8m (2yd) length of 2cm (¾in) wide florist's ribbon and leaving a 46cm (18in) tail bend it into 3 or 4 loops about 20cm (8in) wide, leaving another 46cm (18in) tail. Fold a length of stub wire in half over the centre of the loops and twist it to secure the bow. Insert at the top of the ball to hide the hook and leave the ends trailing down the ball.

10 Hang the ball A piece of nylon fishing line will make an invisible thread to hang the ball. Alternatively a length of ribbon or wire bound with ribbon will do equally well. Mist the arrangement with water every day to keep it looking fresh.

Daisy ball
A simple, but effective, hanging ball can be made using only one type of flower. A bunch of chrysanthemums would make a 'daisy' ball.

Roses and peonies

The garden comes into its own in the summer, with the herbaceous borders and roses at their best. Arranging old-fashioned flowers picked from your own garden is the nicest way to bring this summer feeling into your home, but you can capture the beauty of a bountiful garden wherever you live, because roses, peonies, sweet peas and other summer flowers are sold by florists.

Whether picking or buying, for a convincing natural look, try to include flowers in many stages of maturity: tight bud, half open and fully open, but not over mature. (Florists may give a discount for half-open blooms; it's worth asking.) Including just a few unusual flowers or sprigs of foliage, whether from your own garden, attractive weeds picked from a roadside, or long stemmed parsley or rosemary from a greengrocer, helps to personalize the floral display enormously.

Suggested quantities and colours are given for the following arrangements,
but you can vary them, according to taste, budget and availability. One stunning option, for a floral display, would be a single colour scheme, such as pink or creamy white.

Preparing the vase For both these arrangements you will need a block of florist's foam cut vertically in half. Saturate the block in water, then impale it on a florist's prong and fix it to a base with mastic (see page 14). The base can be a shallow bowl or a plate with a lip.

Budding beauty

This sumptuous display is front facing and rounded, rather like an all-round arrangement cut vertically in half. Florists usually strip most peony foliage from the stems as part of conditioning, but you can ask your florist in advance to leave the foliage on. Alternatively you could use florist's laurustinus, ruscus, or seasonal garden foliage instead.

▲ A welcome sight
Brighten up the hallway with a floral display. Here this white and pink bouquet provides a wonderful welcome.

Materials
12 pale pink double peonies
3 deep pink double peonies
1 white double peony
4 white stocks
5 cream roses
1 bunch **astrantia** (masterwort)
1 bunch **mixed sweet peas**

Coaxing rose buds open
Re-cut the stems, place the buds in warm water in a warm spot, such as near an airing cupboard or radiator, or sit the jug of buds in a hot bath.

1 **Setting the display height** Insert a stock centrally and well back, then a shorter peony either side of the stock, 2 peonies in the front and 1 on each side. This gives the globe-shaped framework. Save any cut off peony stems with foliage attached.

▲ *Rose cluster*
This magnificent display of roses would look wonderful as the table centrepiece at a garden party, or for any special occasion. For a change you could use yellow roses, rather than red, and add a sunny touch.

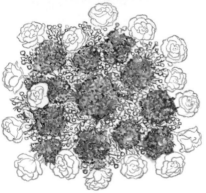

2 **Keeping it round** With an imaginary hemisphere in mind, insert the remaining peonies, placing the white one centrally. Vary the stem lengths, but with none longer than the 'framework' peonies. Angle the stems towards the centre, so all the flowers appear to originate from a single point. Insert the remaining stocks to fill. Cut the 5 rose stems to varying lengths, and insert 3 to form a diagonal line in the centre front, the remaining 2 angled in the opposite way, to form a rough 'V'.

Rose delights

This admittedly extravagant all-round display would make a stunning centrepiece for a summer wedding buffet table. On a tight budget, use fewer roses and more gypsophila or sea lavender, or short-stemmed, 'sweetheart' roses, which come in many lovely colours, including a subtle, pale creamy champagne. Silver artemisia adds a lacy finishing touch, but is short lived once cut, so add it at the very last minute.

Materials
3 large bunches **gypsophila**
30-36 **pink roses**
30-36 **red roses**
12 stems **trachelium** (throatwort)
6 sprigs **artemisia** foliage

2 **Filling the outline** Break the gypsophila into branches and insert, to create an evenly dense, rounded mass, working from the roses to the top trachelium. Cut the remaining trachelium slightly shorter than the roses. Insert here and there, to add colour contrast and density.

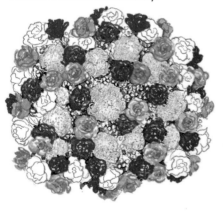

3 **Inspecting the display** Look at it from the top and sides as well as front, inserting the sweet peas and astrantias, in separate clusters, to fill any gaps. Tuck in reserved sprigs of peony or other foliage to hide the florist's foam block.

1 **Setting the heights** Place a trachelium centrally, and then set the circumference with pink and red roses inserted round the sides, like the spokes of a wheel, but at slightly varying levels.

3 **Inserting the remaining roses** Work with the pink and red together to fill out an imaginary globe. Space them roughly equally apart, and to stand slightly proud of the gypsophila and trachelium. Turn the arrangement round as you work, to make sure it is evenly covered.

4 **Finishing touch** Immediately before the arrangement goes on display, insert the artemisia foliage, filling any gaps.

Oranges and lemons

Decking the hall with boughs of holly is the obvious choice for Christmas decorations, but evergreens can look more interesting if brightly coloured fruit such as rosy apples, oranges and lemons are added to the display. Nuts too can be added, to enhance the arrangement. Although this may seem extravagant since the fruit and nuts can't be eaten, it is much cheaper than buying fresh flowers at this time of year, and far more original.

Whether you prefer a discreet display to hang at the window, a grand swag to drape by the hearth or a deluxe dinner table centrepiece for a festive party, you can make them all at home quickly and easily following these instructions.

▼ *Bells of St Clements*
These three posies look impressive, but they are really easy to make. Each ball, made of florist's foam, is wired so that a hanging string can be secured to it. Next, the surface is covered with evergreen, and finally wired-up fruit (see page 43) are added. Paper bows add the finishing touch to the hanging posies.

▲ Fireside favourite

This super swag adds visual warmth to this cosy decor. The scene is set to light the fire, roast the chestnuts and settle down to a relaxing evening.

Colourful ideas

Evergreen arrangements look wonderful and are cheap to make, especially if the holly and ivy are picked from your own garden. Here, festive fruit and pine cones add extra zest to the swag.

MAKING THE SWAG

Materials

Florist's foam and chicken wire frame (available from your local florist)
Moss enough to cover the whole swag
Evergreens such as **holly**, **ivy** and **yew**
9 Oranges
10 Apples
7 fir cones
Secateurs, stub wires and **florist's wire**
Burgundy red velvet 2m (80in) in length, 20cm (8in) wide

1 Preparing the framework If the swag is for a special place, measure up to find the length of swag you require and trim the foam and wire frame to size. Most florists sell frames in standard sizes. Remember when covered with foliage the swag will be much larger.

2 Wiring up the fruit Push two 30cm (12in) stub wires at right angles horizontally through the base of each fruit. Then twist all the wire ends together so that the wires form a single stem. Wire up all the fruit following the same method.

3 Preparing the cones Wire up the fir cones by wrapping a length of wire around the base of each cone and then twisting the two ends together in a similar way to the fruit, ending up with a stalk of wire. Wire all the cones using the same method.

4 Attach a hanging hook Eventually the swag will have a front and back. At what will be the back of the swag twist a length of florist's wire around the frame attaching the wire at both ends and leaving a loop in the middle. This is to hang the swag to a wall hook.

5 Starting off With right sides together fold the velvet fabric in half lengthways and seam down the long edge. Turn right side out to form a roll. Twist the velvet roll around the swag working from the top down. Attach the two ends at the swag back with wire pins.

6 Adding moss Cover the swag with moss, using 10cm (4in) lengths of florist's wire folded in half to attach the moss. To make the velvet look interesting cover some of it with moss and fluff other sections out. Then, hang the swag up so that fruit and foliage can be added at the right angle.

7 Adding the fruit Once the fruit has been wired it should be simple to just push it into the arrangement. Arrange the fruit at various intervals over the swag, clumping each type of fruit together to give bright areas of a similar colour. Once finished, stand back to check the effect.

8 Attaching the cones Seven large cones have been used for this arrangement. They have been interspersed between the velvet and the fruit at various intervals. Once the cones have been wired they can be simply pushed into the mossy swag. Again, step back to check the effect.

9 Finishing off Push sprigs of holly and ivy into the swag to add an extra festive touch. Again, stand back to check the effect and move any sprigs you are unhappy with. Once you are pleased with the effect, hang the swag by the side of the fireplace on a wall hook. Or place the swag along the shelf.

Table Topping

This delightful table display can be made in a jiffy by placing a bowl of fruit in the centre of a shop bought wreath. If the wreath is rather simple you can add nuts, Christmas baubles and even lighted candles to make it look impressive. However, it's cheaper and far more fun to make your table arrangement with material gathered from your garden.

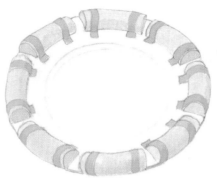

MAKING A FRUIT BOWL

Materials
Large plate
Laurel leaves
Selection of evergreens
Cones
Sphagnum moss
Fruit, **lemons, limes, tangerines, apples, dried apricots, kiwis, kumquats** and **plums**
Nuts, **walnuts, Brazil nuts**
Florist's foam
Stub wires
Reel of wire
Florist's tape
Scissors

1 Starting off Tape similar sized pieces of florist's foam around the rim of a large plate. Arrange the foam pieces so that they are close, but not overlapping. This will form the base of the arrangement.

2 Building up Secure laurel leaves into the foam all around the edge of the plate. Then use various evergreens such as variegated holly, ivy cypress leaves and fir to totally cover the foam to make a decorative edging to the plate. Add the wired up pine cones for extra interest and fill in any gaps with moss.

3 Finishing off Carefully arrange the fruit and nuts in the centre of the plate, stacking the smaller fruit on top. Fill in any gaps with the dried apricots, laurel and ivy leaves to add the finishing touch.

▼ Getting fruity
This wonderful arrangement is certainly good enough to eat, and will make a stunning centrepiece for a special dinner party, or your home at Christmas. Its surprisingly quick and easy to make, but once finished it looks as if it took ages to design and prepare.

Informal arrangements

Light-hearted and relaxed, casual flower arrangements are increasingly popular, and today many top-quality florists offer informal displays, as well as the more formal traditional and symmetrical ones.

Although casual flower arrangements may appear accidental or spontaneous and lack the obvious, tight control and geometry of a formal display, this doesn't mean that you can just throw a bunch of flowers into a vase and hope for the best.

Informal arrangements need as much thought and care as more structured ones, though it's often a question of going by instinct, trying out the flowers first in one way, then another, until the effect looks just right. Try to avoid symmetry, when one half mirrors the other, and explosive-type displays, when all stems radiate tightly out from a central point. Though the traditional rules – no stem should cross another, for example, and the tallest flower should be 1½ times the height of the vase – don't apply, if an arrangement looks awkward or crammed in, take it apart and try again.

Decide on the setting and the colours you like, whether a monochromatic scheme of pink, white or yellow, a soft pastel scheme, or a colourful, carnival mix. Give yourself plenty of time to experiment, and try to have plenty of raw material to hand, including extra foliage, to create a generously full effect. If the arrangement is to be seen from all sides, turn it around as you build it up, for an even display.

▼ Country-casual charm
Honeysuckle, cow parsley, lady's mantle and catmint fill an old-fashioned, traditional-style blue-and-white jug. Note that the flowers have been encouraged to spill over, hiding the top of the jug.

▲ In the pink
Hyacinths, narcissi, anemones, poppies, Turk's-cap, ranunculus and tulips sit in separate vases.

▼ Opulent effect
Peonies, campanulas, dill, delphiniums and masterwort create a vibrant summer arrangement.

Informal flowers

A container generously full of a single type of flower, such as tulip or daisy, can be as informal as a freshly picked posy of dozens of different sprigs. Old-fashioned, country garden flowers, such as peonies, wallflowers, shasta daisies, delphiniums and flag irises, and common wildflowers, such as cow parsley and buttercups, are ideal. Luckily, florists carry cheap and cheerful, old-fashioned garden flowers, such as pot marigolds, sweet peas and sweet Williams, in season, so if you do not have the flowers in your own garden you can buy them ready-cut and pretend that you've picked them yourself.

If you do need to rely on formal florists' flowers, such as long-stemmed hybrid-tea roses, gladioli and chrysanthemums, you can still create an informal display by combining them with garden material; the unexpected combination of florists' and garden flowers can be especially exciting, while still diffusing the formal effect of the florists' flowers. Alternatively, place formal florists' flowers in a casual container – an old enamel coffee pot, for example, or decorative tea caddy. With florists' flowers, try to choose single, daisy-like chrysanthemums and spray carnations, rather than the single-stemmed varieties. With a little practice you can tell the flowers that will make the best informal displays in your home.

Informal containers

Almost anything that holds water can be an informal container. Kitchenware and simple stoneware containers are ideal, or plastic-lined wicker baskets. Transparent glass containers are lovely, but they are unsuitable for use with foundations such as florists' foam block or crumpled wire mesh netting. With clear glass, you have to rely on the stems supporting each other. Alternatively, wedge them with pebbles or other attractive objects such as fruit like the lemons which are shown on page 48.

Costly, ornate china, crystal or silver vases, or those with Classical, urn-like outlines, tend to have formal overtones, but you could fill them with a casual display of yellow garden flowers, such as a huge bunch of simple buttercups, for a little visual joke.

Consider the larger setting. You can quickly enhance a casual display by surrounding it with a collection of china, pottery, wickerwork or glassware, repeating the theme of the container. And as well as single containers, you can group a few small containers, each filled with a single type of flower or a pleasant mixture, for a jolly display.

MAKING A DISPLAY

This magnificent informal arrangement contrasts beautifully with its formal setting. The gold mirror frames the display, while visually doubling it.

Although the types and numbers of flowers used are set out below, recreating an exact replica isn't necessary, as long as you get a good mix of flower shapes and colours, and make the display generously full. Larkspur, for example, could be substituted for the delphiniums; scabious for the poppies; sweet peas for the lisianthus; pinks for the roses; and ivy for the hops.

▶ Cunningly casual
Although this arrangement is placed in a formal setting, it can be thrown together easily with summer blooms.

Materials
Container
Saturated florists' foam block
2 delphiniums
1 bunch antirrhinums
3 peonies
2 lilies
1 phlox
1 bunch lady's mantle
2 poppies
1 bunch iris
Golden hop stems
Roses
Lisianthus

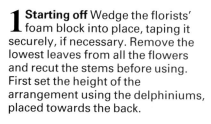

1 Starting off Wedge the florists' foam block into place, taping it securely, if necessary. Remove the lowest leaves from all the flowers and recut the stems before using. First set the height of the arrangement using the delphiniums, placed towards the back.

2 Adding flowers Use the antirrhinums to set the width and begin the central infill. Insert the peonies to form a triangle. Add bulk with the iris and clumps of lady's mantle, to continue the infill. Make one clump larger than the other, to avoid symmetry.

3 Finishing off Insert one tall lily stem off centre, and a shorter one, low down and centrally. Add the poppies, phlox and lisianthus. Tuck the stems of the hops off centre, just above the rim, and roses round the rim, lightly massaging their stems to create soft curves.

47

▲ Autumn contrast
Hydrangeas, rose hips, hot-pink nerines and euonymus branches in berry counteract the formality of long-stemmed roses. The glass vase means that the stems also become part of the display.

▶ Acid yellow
Double yellow tulips, wedged in place with fresh lemons, fill a glass cube vase, decorated with raffia-tied twigs. The tulip leaves have been left to provide greenery, while the twigs impart a natural feel.

Watch the outline
Aim for an airy, irregular silhouette, rather than a hard, dense globe of flowers and foliage. Using 1, 3, 5 or 7 of any one type of flower of various sizes will help to create a natural asymmetry.

Floating flowers

One of the easiest forms of flower arrangement is simply to float the heads on water in a bowl or dish. They can be arranged in any size of container, from a small saucer to a large dish, and they make perfect centrepieces for a dining table – low enough not to block the conversation across the table. Small floating arrangements would also look pretty set on a windowsill, dressing table or hall table – any position where they are viewed from above.

Almost any flowers are suitable – this is an ideal way of using the last few fresh flower heads in an almost dead arrangement, or those flower heads in full bloom which have been bent or

broken off in the garden by boisterous children and animals. Even single flower petals and leaves can be floated on the water or sprinkled over the finished display.

If your flower heads have short stalks you can fix them in position by filling the container with plain glass marbles topped up with water. These are available from florists and are used in flower arranging to hold stems in position. They look particularly attractive glistening in a glass container.

These arrangements have a limited life so keep them simple and inexpensive, changing them before the petals get sodden and go brown.

▲ Wild and garden flowers
Flowers with heads of tiny blooms such as meadowsweet or cow parsley make an ideal framework. Campanulas, Peruvian lilies, daisies, violas, pelargoniums and oxalis are set in heads of meadowsweet. Below, a single head fits into a small bowl with flowers inserted between.

▲ Two-tiered effect
A small bowl set in the centre of a large plate contains an arrangement of every shade and type of pink pelargonium. The smaller blooms fill the central bowl, while the larger blossoms are less tightly packed around the plate allowing the pattern of the china to show through.

◄ A simple dish
No real attempt has been made to arrange these flower heads apart from keeping to shades of pink and mauve, and leaving the attractively patterned border of the dish clear. The flowers include delphiniums, pelargoniums and hydrangeas and the effect is fresh and natural.

► On the diagonal
Formal lines of white hyacinths and yellow kerria blooms and leaves are fitted across this square dish to make a bold display in bright colours. Bluebell florets have been used to fill any spaces and the corners.

An autumn arrangement

Autumn, with its rich golden and red colours and harvest imagery, is a splendid season for making your own indoor flower arrangements, and even without flowers you can still create really impressive displays, such as the one shown.

Pot et fleur, French for pot and flower, is the technique of combining cut material, whether flowers or, as here, leaves and berries, with any favourite house plant in a stunning but temporary display.

With pot et fleur, the plants provide a permanent supply of green or more colourful filler material, and cut flowers or branches of foliage are added to ring the changes.

It's an economical way of creating impressive arrangements, since you can re-use the house plants again and again, and a little cut flowers or branches of foliage go a long way.

The more house plants you have, the wider your range of pot et fleurs, so try to build up a collection of different house plants, especially as some grow quickly, providing even more mass, virtually for free.

Foliage, flowers and pot plants

Foliage As well as the oak leaves shown, other colourful autumn foliage includes amelanchier, beech, hazel, birch, maple and many deciduous azaleas. Once leaves turn colour, however, they can no longer take up water, so expect to replace them with fresh branches every few days.

Another solution would be to use glycerined foliage, which has autumnal tones and a supple texture, but is already fully preserved. Glycerined foliage branches should not need replacing either.

Flowers Cotoneaster in berry is shown, but firethorn, barberry, snowberry, mahonia, hawthorn and even rose hips are equally suitable, with berries ranging from white to yellow, orange, pink, scarlet, purple and blue black. For high drama, use leafless branches of crab apple or rowan.

If you want to include cut flowers with autumnal overtones, chrysanthemums, Michaelmas daisies, Guernsey lilies, kaffir lilies, dahlias and gladioli are all ideal.

Plants Virtually any house plant with a small rootball can be used in a pot et fleur, from the trailing devil's ivy to coloured-leaved begonias and crotons,

ferns, bromeliads, ivy or coleus potted up from the garden.

Seasonal house plants, such as pot 'mums' or cyclamen, combine the natural attraction of flowers with longevity, providing weeks of colour.

Whatever pot plants you choose, remember to water and feed them while they're hidden in the display.

It's also a good idea to rotate the plants you use in pot et fleurs, so they can recuperate in the temperature and light conditions that suit them best between their 'tours of duty'.

▲ A vibrant display
The focal point of this mixed foilage house plant arrangement is a blushing bromeliad. Different pot plants will provide alternative colour themes, so you can easily alter the emphasis to tone in with your home.

MAKING THE ARRANGEMENT

This front-facing display features oak and cotoneaster cut from the garden, and five small house plants. If you have no garden, your florist can get glycerined beech or oak, and cotoneaster may be available. Wild blackberry or elderberry stems are another option.

Try to use branches that grow in flat sprays, rather than bushy ones. At a pinch, you can introduce the berry theme with berried house plants, such as winter cherry.

An eight-sided, Oriental vase is used, but any wide-necked, waterproof container deep enough to hold the rootballs is fine. Stoneware, lined wicker baskets or even orange ovenware containers would reinforce the theme.

Materials

A wide Oriental-style bowl or any vase of your choice
Florist's foam, and **peat**
5 branches of oak, 4 cotoneaster branches
Small potted plants: 1 medium miniature palm, 1 medium weeping fig, 2 dracaena plants (1 white, 1 pink), **1 medium blushing bromeliad** and **sphagnum moss**

1 Start the display If necessary, raise the levels inside the container with damp peat or sections of saturated florist's foam block, roughly cut to fit, so the surface of the rootballs come 2.5cm (1in) below the rim of the container. Some pots may be deeper than others.

2 Adding the plants Place the plants, still in their pots, in the container. Place the palm in the centre, the weeping fig behind, the variegated dracaenas to the left and right and, finally, the blushing bromeliad in front. Raise and tilt the bromeliad, so it faces towards the front and overhangs the rim, forming the focal point.

3 Adding the florist's foam To keep the plants in place and support the branches, tightly pack the space between the pots of the pot plants and the sides of the container with slabs of saturated florist's foam, roughly cut to fit. The larger the pieces of florist's foam, the more stable the overall effect will be.

4 Start framing the plants Remove the lowest leaves from 5 oak branches, and insert them in the florist's foam around the rim, to frame the plants. Use the tallest branches at the back and shorter ones in the front, to help conceal the pots and foundation.

5 Finishing off Remove the lowest leaves and berries from 4 cotoneaster branches, and insert them here and there in the florist's foam, filling in spaces between the oak branches. For a tidy, professional-looking finish, cover the surface with sphagnum moss.

Table decorations

These wonderful little flower trees always look good and are fun to make. To create a dramatic impact use dark colours like the deep red roses and bottle green ivy, here. For a softer, more romantic look use paler coloured blooms, and variegated ivy.

If you intend to give the tree as a gift or you want to make it for a special occasion, plan the arrangement in advance. This flower tree should stay fresh for several days, but for a longer lasting arrangement use dried flowers and lichen moss to cover the ball.

▼ *Double delight*
These lovely rose trees help to make any occasion really special. Here, they are used to grace the side table at a wedding, but they could be used as the centre-piece at almost any important event.

Materials

Waterproof terracotta pot
Florist's foam You need two pieces, a
large square block and a **medium ball**

Green ivy Try to buy a bunch of ivy with
berries attached
12 deep red roses
Lichen moss

Gypsophila
Contorted willow Choose a firm piece
Leaf shine and **craft knife**
Wired ribbon and **florist's wire**

MAKING A ROSE TREE

1 Making the base Soak the florist's
foam in water. Then fill the pot
with some stones to weight it and
add the foam block; arrange this to
stand above the rim of the pot. With a
craft knife shave the contorted willow
at both ends making two sharp
points. Place one sharpened end into
the foam and secure using five
hairpin shaped florist wires. Check the
willow is secure with a gentle tug.

2 Shaping the tree Cover the foam
block with the moss, attaching the
moss using more hairpin shaped
wire. Make sure both the willow and
moss are firmly fixed at this stage.
Now add the foam ball to the top
spike of the contorted willow,
pushing it firmly into place. Again,
secure with florist's wire, as for the
base, then check the fixing is secure
with a gentle tug.

3 Adding the ivy Using the firm
stems of the ivy leaves skewer
them into the foam ball, forming a
ring around the outline, thus splitting
the ball visually in half. Fill one half
of the ball with ivy. Then, after
checking to ensure there are no large
gaps, repeat for the other side. Twist
wire around the soft stems of the ivy
berries and fix into the ball between
the leaves.

4 **Positioning the roses** Place four roses around the outline of the ball, again, visually splitting the ball in half. Then add four roses to each side of the ball making sure they are evenly spaced between the berries and each other. As rose stalks are fairly firm, they need not be wired.

5 **Attaching the gypsophila** Before adding the gypsophila, spray the tree with leaf shine. Because the gypsophila is fragile the stems need wiring. For a formal effect use only a small amount of gypsophila, as here. A softer, misty look can be achieved by adding more.

6 **Finishing off** Finally add a bow. Wind the ribbon to make four loops and secure in place with florist's wire twisted around the middle. Tie a second length of ribbon over the wire for tails. Use the twisted ends of florist's wire to secure bow at the base of the ball.

Alternative designs

Once you have made up one flower tree you will soon realise you can use all kinds of fresh and dried flowers to make others.

Fresh flowers Almost any kind of flower can be fixed into the ball, although roses are particularly popular. Try using seasonal garden flowers like daisy chrysanthemums, wallflowers or tulips.

Dried flowers Again, almost all dried flowers can be used in these tree arrangements, but compact flower heads work best. Dried roses, statice and nigella all work especially well. If you are making a dried flower tree make sure you use the appropriate florist's foam.

Foliage The best foliage to use is ivy, which comes in either a plain or variegated form. Plain ivy is quite dark, so if you want a lighter effect and are using paler flowers it is a good idea to opt for a

▶ *Never a wallflower?*
Here, a tree made from red, yellow and orange wallflowers, a rustic pole, and bun moss makes a stunning display, on an ornate sideboard, in front of a mirror. The lighted candles add to the light effects in the room.

variegated form. Other types of popular foliage to use include privet, euonymus and yew.

Fruit Berries, small apples and even nuts can be added to these trees to give a more ornamental air, provided they are wired securely. You can make the arrangements look more like little fruit trees by using the leaves as well.

Stem Many different types of wood can be used for the stem of the tree; contorted willow is probably the most popular because it has a lovely twisted effect. Gnarled vine is also often used. However, if desperate, an old broom handle might even rise to the occasion if the stem is decorated.

An effective idea, is to paint the stem with a brightly coloured paint. Otherwise, try wrapping the stem with ribbons and tying a pretty bow.

Pots There are masses of pots on the market and each type will influence the look of the arrangement, so exercise great care when choosing the pot for your tree. If, you have difficulty finding a particular colour, you can always paint one to match your flowers.

◀ *Rambling roses*
This natural looking rose tree can be made in a similar way to the others but the honeysuckle, jasmine, Sedum spectabile and mini-roses have longer stems. A wicker basket at the base adds a pretty touch.

Floral napkin rings

A beautifully laid table always makes a dinner party memorable simply because the guests feel they are being cherished. It's finishing touches that turn any meal into a special occasion, like these hand-made floral napkin rings which are quite exquisite; yet they can be made for next to nothing using seasonal flowers and leaves picked from your garden or bought cheaply. Add floral napkin rings to your table next time you have friends round for a meal and watch their delight and surprise.

It's probably best to practise making the napkin rings before the event, especially if you're making them for an important occasion, then you can check out the techniques and see how long it takes you to make them.

It is a good idea to prepare your floral napkin rings as close as possible to the meal time to avoid wilting. To keep them fresh, moisten by spraying them with a gardener's mist, then store the rings, sealed in a plastic bag, in a cool place; the fridge is ideal.

Plain tableware will highlight your handiwork. White plates are superb for display purposes. Pastel shades will also look good, assuming the colours of the foliage and the plates don't clash with each other. Try to avoid using really bright crockery, as it may overpower the pale floral tones. Stand back to check the effect when you have laid the table. Some items may detract the eye from the rings – change these.

You can experiment by making napkin rings to match your favourite napkins. Toning shades of the same

▲ Simply stunning
This delightful napkin ring is splendid, and it's one of the easiest to make. A grapevine ring, which can be bought in most garden shops, forms the basic framework then two pink peony blooms and several lavender stalks are simply attached with wire.

colour always work well; pink rose buds look wonderful with a paler pink napkin. While yellow napkins look brilliant with darker yellows and oranges found in nasturtium blooms. Alternatively work with contrasting colours like yellow napkins with blue grape hyacinths.

To keep costs low, always choose flowers which are in season and when there are few available work with evergreen leaves, like ivy.

Materials
90cm (36in) ivy cut into 3 lengths
Florist's wire

▼ *Sculptured leaves*

MAKING THE IVY RING

1 Making a ring Using one length of ivy, twist it to form a ring of about 20cm (8in) round and attach one end to the main stem with florist's wire.

2 Adding extra ivy Secure the other end to the circle of ivy about halfway round. Then twist the remaining lengths of ivy around the circle ensuring it covers the ring.

3 Finishing off Once you are happy with the arrangement use florist's wire to hold the ivy stems together. Then place your napkin through its ring arranging the ivy decoratively.

Materials
Gladioli flower on a stalk and **gladioli leaf** 30cm (10in) long
Scissors

▼ *Style on a budget*

MAKING THE LEAF TIE

1 Soaking the leaf Check the leaf is long enough by wrapping it around the napkin. Make the leaf easy to work with by soaking it in warm water.

2 Knotting up Allow the leaf to soak for about an hour before drying it thoroughly. Wrap the leaf around the napkin and tie it in a loose knot, taking care not to damage it.

3 Trimming off Use the scissors to trim off the ends of the leaf at an angle. Then add the gladioli bloom to the napkin ring by placing the stalk through the leaf circle.

Materials

Gypsophila, delphiniums and **euphorbia** in small bunches, or single flowers so that they are easy to wire.
Green gutta percha tape
Florist's wire 20cm (8in) long

MAKING THE FLORAL BAND

1 Binding the wire Select and trim the flowers. Bind the tape around the wire pulling it taut so that it sticks. Form the end into a hoop.

2 Fixing in place Bind tape to the wire for about 5cm (2in), then begin to fix the flowers in place, binding each stem in a continuous operation, twisting as you work.

3 Finishing off Work a tight arrangement in a 12cm (5in) length, and bind the wire with tape. Bend and hook wire into a ring.

◄ *Summer scents*

Materials

18 pieces of **bear grass** approximately 40cn (16in) in length
Scissors

▼ *Love knots*

MAKING THE GRASS RING

1 Sorting the grass Arrange the grass so that it all lines up at the bottom, then roll the napkin loosely lengthwise rather than folding it.

2 Aligning the grass Carefully tie the grass in a simple knot ensuring that the grasses are still aligned at the base and fanning out at the top.

tip

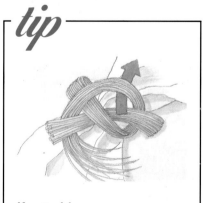

Knotty ideas
For a larger knot, tie another on top of the first; but the grasses must be longer.

Materials
Silver birch twigs
Florist's wire
Selection of **red berries** with **leaves** and **2 or 3 eucalyptus berries.**
Scissors

MAKING THE BERRY RING

1 Twisting twigs Bend the twigs into a circle of the correct size depending on the thickness of your napkin. Then bind using the florist's wire, to ensure the twigs are secure.

2 Testing the ring Repeat with a second circle of twigs and wire both circles together. Test again to ensure that the twigs are secure.

3 Attaching berries Bind the berries and leaves with florist's wire and use it to attach them to the ring in a 12cm (5in) length, building up a cluster.

4 Finishing off Finally bind the 2 or 3 eucalyptus berries with florist's wire and use them to fill in spaces. Ensure they are secure.

tip

Table manners
Avoid using poisonous material in any floral arrangements on a dining table, particularly if small children are likely to be guests. Suitable berries include red and black currants, blueberries, gooseberries, firm raspberries and small strawberries.

▼ *Berry bright*